Pimp Game

109

Born

To

Mack

itbftr@yahoo.com

TJ Clemons

Introduction

This is the last installation of the pimping game. Look for one

more compilations that will include all the books in my series

combined into one Platinum Pimps and Players Edition. I have

been bringing this game to you for a few years. But due to the

many changes that are going on in my life it is time to move on

to another chapter in my life. I will still be writing books and I

sincerely hope that you have enjoyed taking this journey with me

into the world of pimping, pandering, and prostitution. This

chapter of my life has come to an end and many more are

waiting to be written. Game Over! Now my new life begins.

Thank you for all your love and support. The history of my

voyage is forever set in stone. The game lives on. The game will

never die but it will continue to innovate, expand, and evolve.

And the players will change. Once one individual leaves the game

another one is being groomed into the role as a pimp and a

player. Check out all of my books online because I will continue

to write more as long as the motivation is still there. I have an

extensive body of work that will be appreciated for generations

after I'm long gone. Respect the game or the game will disrespect

you. Embrace the game and the game will embrace you. There

are rules and regulations that have passed down for many years.

On the Stroll

Pimp: "Bitch how much money do you have for my pockets?"

Whore: "I just woke up daddy!"

Pimp: "Bitch we got a mother fucking problem then because I

don't have any money in my pockets either. I came out here to

collect on my check. Bitch you better go make some money right

the fuck now!"

Whore: "It's cold out here!"

Pimp: "I don't care how cold it is! You better go out there and get

my mother fucking money because ain't shit in life free out here!

Take care of your mother fucking business before I take care of it

for you and put my foot in your ass! Get your ass in and out of

these cars the way you are supposed to be doing."

Another Pimp: "Bitch you look highly qualified! What are you

doing out here in the cold? Come sit in my car and let me warm

warm you up!"

Another Whore: "I already have a man!"

Another Pimp: "What do you mean you have a man?"

Another Whore: "He is on his way over here right now!"

Another Pimp: "You're going to be my bitch. It's time to make a move in my direction then. You owe me some money hoe! Bitch get over here! Don't make me get off this corner. I ain't going to sweat you but I am get let you have a chance to choose up! It's a limited time offer so you better make your mind up real quick!"

Another Whore: "I'm down with my man that's my plan!"

Another Pimp: "You better call him right now and tell him that you owe me some mother fucking money!"

Trick: 'Look at that big mother fucking ass! Give me some of that

pussy! Let me see that ass! Come here girl let me spank that ass!'

Prostitute: "You don't know what to do with this!"

Trick: "Yes I do! Come here baby! Let me get some of that pussy!

What's up girl? I have a pocket full of money for you!"

Prostitute: "You ain't talking about nothing. I'm about to move on

up the block and find a man that can cash me out. I have the

best pussy. Holler at me when you're ready for an upgrade."

Trick: "I'm serious baby. I want some of that sweet candy!

Let me get up in that pussy! I'll lick it like a lollipop!"

Pimp: "How much money do you have for me?"

Whore: "Daddy I just broke luck and got some cash! $200."

Pimp: "As long as you been out here that's all the money that you

have bitch? I left your ass out here a long time ago bitch! "

Whore: "Yes daddy!"

Pimp: "Bitch you better get on down this street and make

something happen right the fuck now! Go get me some more

money before I kick you in your ass! I ain't got time for that

shit bitch! You better get your shit together! Get on down the

street and don't look back! You punk ass bitch! I'm about to go

get me a swan. White bitches let you pimp and the black hoes make you pimp! I'm tired of this shit! I'm gone knock off a

white bitch tonight if you don't get your shit together! I need

my money bitch! Right now, my pockets are looking really bad.

Bitch I ain't got a mother fucking thing to show dealing with

your funky ass! You play too mother fucking much hoe!

One of these white bitches are going to fuck with my pimping!

And I bet you she is going to let me pimp her without a mother

fucking attitude!"

Mack: "How much you got for me baby girl?

Whore: "I want to talk to you about that daddy! My money has

been a little tight with you. And I have been thinking about

rolling with Shorty the pimp!"

<Mack pimps smack the bitch back to reality!>

Mack: "You can be with Shorty if you want to bitch! But

everything on this track belongs to me! Bitch your time is up!

Now break your mother fucking purse before I have to put my

hands on you again! Bitch is this all the mother fucking money

that you have for a pimp? You sorry as excuse for a whore!"

Mack's Whore: "Hey daddy, are you waiting on me?"

Mack: "Bitch you should have been waiting on me! But if you

knew better then, you would do better!"

Shorty: "I been looking for you bitch! Where the fuck is my

money? You got me out here looking like a mother fucking fool!"

Whore: "Let me tell you what happened daddy!"

Shorty: "Where is my mother fucking bread at bitch?"

Whore: "That cold mother fucker Mack rolled up on me and took

it right off me! And the mother fucker had the nerve to pimp

smack me like I was his bitch!"

Shorty: "Wrong answer bitch!"

<Shorty pimp smacks her hard! And she falls to the concrete.>

Shorty: "Bitch you better get your punk ass off of the ground and get my mother fucking money before I break my foot off in your whore ass! You better act like you represent me out here and stop playing bitch! Every time I turn around one of these mother fucking funky ass bitches is thinking that I'm playing! I ain't got time for none of this bullshit!"

Pimp partner: "What are you doing out here player?"

Mack: "I'm mother fucking pimping!"

Pimp partner: "I feel you on that player! Do your thang!"

Mack: "It ain't nothing but a chicken wing player! This pimp game is serious. I had to blow down on one of Shorty's bitches and get some mother fucking paper out of her."

Pimp partner: "You know that mother fucker is crazy as fuck and walks around with that switch blade if something goes down!"

Mack: "Fuck Shorty! If that mother fucker has a problem with me then we can go ahead and jump into some gangster shit! I'm too prepared to be mother fucking scared!"

In the Beginning

<Mack is in a hotel room and hears a knock at his door.>

Ole Pimp: "Look mother fucker when I'm dealing with my bitch

I need peace and mother fucking quiet! Do you understand? And

if you have a problem with that then move to another room!"

Mack: "Then tell that bitch over there to keep it down!"

Ole Pimp: "That's my mother fucking bitch and she is going to

make as much noise as I tell her to! You got that chump?"

<Mack pulls out a gun on the Ole Pimp.>

Mack: "Your time is up! And you better change directions fast!"

Ole Pimp: "My fault young blood. I'm gone tell her to be quiet."

Whore: "That is exactly why I'm leaving your old ass!"

Ole Pimp: "Shut the fuck up bitch! I got this!"

<The whore smacks the pimp over the head with a 40 ounce

bottle and her and Mack start giving him a beat down.>

<The Whore knocks at Mack's door a few hours later after she

gets her belongings out of the nearby hotel room.>

Mack: "I'm going to blow his head clean off of his shoulders!"

Whore: "It's me daddy. I came here to thank you for saving me

from that ancient mother fucking pimp. I have some of the best

pussy that you will ever have the pleasure of experiencing!"

Mack: "You can show me better than you can tell me!"

Whore: "So tell me something. Do you like pussy?"

Mack: "Of course bitch. I love pussy."

Whore: "Have you ever had some good pussy?"

Mack: "All pussy is good. Some is just better than others."

Whore: "Have you ever had this pussy?"

Mack: "Not that I can remember."

Whore: "Then you ain't never had good pussy before."

Mack: "Show me what good pussy is then."

<They make sweet love all night long.>

Whore: "Hey daddy wake up!"

Mack: "Are you talking to me?"

Whore: "I want you to be my pimp!"

Mack: "Pimp?"

Whore: "I want to sell this pussy for you!"

Mack: "I ain't trying to sell that one. I'm trying to keep that one

for myself. You definitely weren't lying. Besides that, I ain't no

mother fucking pimp. I'm a mother fucking hustler!"

Whore: "Look daddy. I'm just trying to help you get on your feet.

Because pimps don't hustle hoes. It's the other way around."

Mack: "So how did you get turned out?"

Whore: "The mother fucker who turned me out was real smooth.

I didn't even know that I was in the game at first. I should have

know that the mother fucker was a pimp because that man was

unreal. His name was Slick."

Mack: "What kind of name was that for a pimp?"

Whore: "Slick was smooth. He made all of us hoes feel like we

was his only bitch. I was so in love with him."

Mack: "Whatever happened to Slick?"

Whore: "This gorilla pimp named Shorty took his main bitch. Then

Slick went to Shorty and cut his throat. But Shorty didn't die. So

Shorty cut Slick's main bitch up with a razor and planted it

Slick for the cops to find. Then Slick went down for murder.

 Why are you looking at your watch?"

Mack: "I'm starting to dig this pimp shit. And it's time for you to

hit the block and start making us some money."

Whore: "You got that right daddy! But pimping ain't easy!"

Mack: "It will be easier with a hoe like you!"

A year into the game

Mack: "I'm pimping now. What's the problem?"

Whore: "I got beat up by a trick!"

Mack: "What happened bitch?"

Whore: "He started beating on me and choking me out talking

about I was cheating on him. I thought I was going to die."

Mack: "Do you know where to find this mother fucker?"

Whore: "He is one of my regulars and I have his number."

Mack: "Well it's about time to give this mother fucker a call.

I'm about to ring his bell because this mother fucker is costing

me money. We are going to give this sick mother fucker a wake

up call that he is never going to forget. Get your phone bitch."

Whore: "Ok daddy! Fuck him up real good!"

Mack: "You best believe this mother fucker is going to feel my

pain and get my pockets right for his mistake. And I bet this

stupid mother fucker has a wife at home that will be interested

in knowing that he is out here fucking whores off the corner."

Whore: "He said my pussy and mouth was 100 times better than the lazy bitch that he has at home. And I make sure that I put it on him really good so that he keeps coming back for more."

Mack: "This silly mother fucker is definitely coming back for more because I'm about to break his pockets like one of my bitches. I'm going all the way in on his ass with no Vaseline!"

Whore: "My pussy is getting wet just thinking about it daddy!"

Mack: "We are going to set his ass up really good. He is fucking with the wrong pimp's money. Now his ass is in a serious trick bag. And I'm going to get this bag off his ass real smooth."

<The whore calls the trick on her cellphone.>

Whore: "Hey honey. I miss my favorite sugar daddy! I'm real

sorry for cheating on you and I want to make it up to you with

a night that you will never forget. Meet me at the hotel that we

always hang out at room 69."

Trick: "I know baby doll. You're my sexy sugar baby. I'll even

bring you a treat if you do a real good job like you always do."

Whore: "I have some new tricks that I have been wanting to try.

I hope you are ready for the ride of your life. Because you are

going to need a seatbelt to hang on. I'm feeling very freakish."

<The trick knocks at room 69 at the local motel.>

Whore: "I'm coming big daddy! I want to look good for you.

The door is open come on in. I'll be in the bathroom freshening

up for you."

Trick: "I'm here baby and I brought you some flowers. I got a

little carried away the last time but I promise to behave myself."

<Mack comes out of the bathroom with a gun in his hand.>

Mack: "You better believe that you are going to have a better

attitude with my bitches. I'm the only mother fucker that puts

his hands on my whores. You are going to learn to stay in a

trick's place. I have something special planned for you today."

Trick: "I'm sorry! I'm sorry I'll make it up to you!"

Mack: "Too late mother fucker! You are about to be sorry

when we get done with your bitch ass. Now break your

mother fucking pockets and put that money in my hand!

And you won't be getting any pussy today mother fucker!"

Trick: "Take the money it's yours just don't hurt me!"

Mack: "You got that right jack. I should fuck you smooth up

but I'm going to let it slide this time because I think that you

have learned a very valuable lesson about putting your hands

on my bitches. I'm going to even let you get with this beautiful

young lady that you damaged. She is no good for me right now.

But I'll let you have the freakiest experience of your trick

life with her after we get something straight."

Trick: "I'll do anything. I just don't want my wife to find out!"

Mack: "That's up to you now. If you don't want her to find out

then it's going to cost you some cold hard cash and a pound of

flesh. You are going to give me $25,000 for all the money that

I'm missing because my best bitch is out of commission."

Trick: "I'll call her and make sure that you get it Mr. Pimp!"

Mack: "I know you will Mr. Trick because I know everything

about you. I know where you live. I know where you work.

I even know where your ugly ass kids got to school. And

I will make sure your lame ass wife gets a taste of some of my

big black dick. You are now my personal ATM machine. If you

miss a payment then I guarantee something bad will happen to

you and your bitch ass wife. I know some big black bulls that

would love to run a train on her and tear that sweet pussy apart."

Trick: "I'll give you anything you want! Just don't come after me,

my wife, or my kids!"

Mack: "Trust and believe me you will break that bread with me or

face the consequences. And from here on out you better respect

the rules of the game and treat these whores like women

because this bitch right here is my personal property.

And just so you know for future reference this bitch is a hoe

and I sent her out here to get my money. So, if any mother

fucker calls, texts, or meets her out here on the streets then

the bitch is fucking. She is supposed to fuck them if she is my

bitch. I should take my razor out and cut you from ear to ear

but I'm not that type of guy especially since your bitch ass

belongs to me now. I'm going to show you some mercy and

keep you warm and safe like I do my other bitches!"

Trick: "Thank you so much Mr. Pimp! I appreciate it."

Mack: "It's all good now it's time for the main event."

Trick: "I won't put my hands on another woman. I promise."

Mack: "I know you won't Mr. Trick because once my bitch puts

this good loving on you, then you are going to learn to respect

any woman that you come across from here on out. Bitch get

the fuck out here! Your sugar daddy is waiting for you!"

Whore: "I'm coming daddy!"

<She walks out wear a 13-inch strap-on dildo.>

Trick: "What is she going to do with that?"

Mack: "She is going to teach you a valuable lesson. Do you see

those handcuffs over there? The ones with the fuzzy pink shit

on them."

Trick: "Yes I see them Mr. Pimp."

Mack: "Grab both pairs and get your ass on the bed!"

Trick: "I don't understand. I thought I was getting some pussy."

Mack: "No she has something else in mind for you today."

Whore: "We are trading places. You are going to be the bitch today. I'm going to fuck the shit out of you literally! Now get on the bed and assume the position. Doggy style!"

Trick: "I thought you was going to please me!"

Mack: "You thought wrong bitch! Now get your ass up on there on the bed and let her handcuff you like a good bitch!"

<Mack pulls the gun on him and orders him on the motel bed.>

Mack: "Hurry up bitch before I change my mind! And by the way

we are going to record this just in case you decide to change

your mind about paying us. All your friends and family members

will get to view it on Facebook. I hope your precious wife and

children never get to find out that the man of their house is a

freak for oversized dildos. I just want my money on time but the

choice is up to you. "

Whore: "Take your clothes off and get your ass on the bed bitch!"

Mack: "It's hammer time!"

Trick: "I'll do it! I'll do it! Just don't tell my wife!"

Mack: "Ok bitch! He is all yours. All you have to do now is say,

Lights! Camera! Action! And press that red record button."

Whore: "OK Daddy! Bitch spread your cheeks and stop crying!"

Trick: "Please be gentle. I have never done this before."

Whore: "I'll treat you just like you did when you were beating

my ass and chocking me out for "cheating" on you!"

Trick: "I'm sorry. I brought you flowers!"

Whore: "Shut up bitch! The more noise that you make the worse

it will be on you. Now get sexy for the camera!"

Trick: "Do you at least have any Vaseline or lube?"

Whore: "I'll spit on it for you if you shut the fuck up bitch!"

Mack: "Ok bitch! It's time to give your sugar daddy the surprise

that he has been waiting for. Get up here and spread your legs

bitch! Put the handcuffs on this woman beating bitch!"

<She handcuffs him to the bed.>

Trick: "You don't have to do this. I'll pay extra if you let me go!"

Mack: "We own you now bitch! You do whatever we tell you to

do. You better be lucky that I'm not putting your ass on the block

with lipstick and a skirt. Just think about that if you get it in your

mind that you don't want to pay me. I'll can get my money out of

your pockets or I can get it out of your ass. I'll have you out here

sucking dick and getting bent the fuck over!"

Trick: "I'll pay. I'll pay. Please don't let her fuck me!"

Mack: "You already fucked up when you put your hands on my

bitch. Now you have to face the consequences of your actions."

Whore: "I'm ready to fuck this bitch daddy!"

Mack: "She is all yours baby girl."

<Mack sets up the camera and presses record!>

Trick: "No! Please don't do it!"

Whore: "Bitch I told you to shut the fuck up! Now I have to go

hard on you. Say hi to the camera. This is your debut movie."

<She proceeds to viciously penetrate and punish him until he

starts crying and passes out from the severe pain. >

Check that bitch

Whore: "The police got your girl Destiny hemmed up in the alley.

They are trying to get some free pussy and head off of her."

Mack: "Check this out. You bitches' better get my money. I'm

sick and tired of excuses. One bitch doesn't shut the track down.

You bitches need to be working extra hard to get that bread.

I need mine. I'm tired of this money coming up short.

These mother fucking pigs got something coming. My bitches

don't fuck for free. Only for a fee."

Police: "Get on your knees bitch!"

Destiny: "Get the fuck out of my face! You smell like bacon."

Police: "I'll bet you get on your knees if I pimp smack you!"

Destiny: "I bet the fuck I won't Porky Pig!"

<Police officer punches her in the stomach and face and she

falls to the ground and tries to get up but the cop only lets her

get up on her knees.>

Police: "You act like you never sucked 2 dicks at the same time."

Officer: "Let's teach this bitch a lesson and take her down to the

police station and run a train on this bitch. Then she might

develop a taste for pork."

Destiny: "Not for all the money in the world. Fuck the police."

<The two police officers take turns pimp smacking her.>

Officer: "This is some good foreplay! Her pussy is good and wet!"

<They both pull out the dicks and try to force her head down.>

Destiny: "What the fuck is this? I don't suck baby dicks!"

<One of the officers pulls out a gun.>

Destiny: "Do you think if you shoot me your dick is going to get bigger? I ain't no mother fucking child molester. Put those little pigs in a blanket away before I bite them off and then the both of you are going to have to get a detective to find your micro dicks!"

Police: "Bitch please! You are a professional. Not only are you

going to suck us both off. You're going to swallow too!"

Destiny: "Get the fuck out of my face before my man fucks

both of you swine smelling mother fuckers up!"

<A car pulls into the alley with bright headlights.>

Officer: "Turn those lights off before I take your ass in! This

is official police business and you are obstructing justice!"

Police: "Turn off your mother fucking headlights now!"

<Mack gets out of the car and walks up to the two cops.>

Mack: "I heard that ya'll was looking for me!"

Police: "Who the fuck are you supposed to be a mother fucking

pimping ass super hero coming to save your little bitch?"

Mack: "You know who I am and what I am. Now you better

gone ahead and turn my bitch loose before I have to jump

into some gangster shit!"

<Mack points his gun at the two police officers.>

Police: "Drop your pistol right now!"

Mack: "No mother fucker I got the jump on you half slick mother

fuckers. I caught you with your pants down and no gun in hand.

You pigs must be book smart because you're definitely not street

smart. Don't turn this into a murder scene!"

Police: "No harm no foul. But we will remember this."

Mack: "Write it down. Take a picture. I don't give a flying fuck!"

Officer: "Do you know how much time you will get if you kill two cops? That's a death penalty case!"

Mack: "Probably none. Because your book smart asses is in the hood doing dirt. Don't nobody around here snitch on cop killers! You mother fuckers better start doing your homework before a pimp like me puts you 6 feet underground! Look at this bitch's face. How is she supposed to work like that? Are you ok Destiny?"

Destiny: "I'm ok but these mother fucks need to go the doctors for their little problem. I have never seen two grown men with little ass baby dicks before!"

Police: "Fuck you bitch!"

Destiny: "Fuck you too small dick mother fuckers!"

Mack: "I'll let you pay me what it's going to cost me because my bitch is out of commission for letting you mother fuckers live another day!"

Officer: "Fuck you and that funky bitch!"

Mack: "I'm tired of playing with you mother fuckers. You got a

pimp out here in the rain and I said break bread!"

Police: "We are the mother fucking law around here!"

Mack: "And I'm a mother fucking vigilante! This is street justice

mother fucker! And your lives can end today! Time is up! I gave

you mother fuckers a chance! Now it's time to meet the man in

the sky!"

Officer: "Hold up! Look in the glove compartment in the front seat

of the car! That's where the money is!"

Mack: "Go get the money bitch!"

Destiny: "Ok Daddy! I found it!"

<Destiny gives Mack the money.>

Mack: "What the fuck is this? Where is the rest of it at?"

Police: "That is the rest mother fucker!"

Mack: "You know what. I gave you pigs a chance!"

Officer: "Look in the trunk under the spare tire!"

Police: "What the fuck are you doing?"

Officer: "Shut the fuck up! I got this!"

Mack: "Good looking out! I'll see you boys around."

Police: "You should have pulled the trigger Mack!"

Paper Chasing

Mack: "Wake your bitch asses up! "

Whore: "What's wrong daddy?"

Mack: "One of your punk ass bitches have been coming up short!"

Whore: "Without Destiny how are we going to make the same?"

Mack: "What the fuck did I tell you when I dropped you off on

the track earlier! I told you to get my mother fucking money!"

Whore: "The police have been on us like white on rice!

What do you want us to do start catching cases?"

Mack: "Catching a case has never stopped a hoe from hoeing!

You act like I ain't never bailed you out before! What's your

mother fucking excuse now?"

Whore: "Shorty had me hemmed up for a while."

Mack: "What the fuck you mean this mother fucker had you in

his half pimping ass face? Bitch you're going to get fucked up!"

Whore: "He was trying to get me to choose him!"

Mack: "And you stood there and listened? You know what time it

is and you know how you are supposed to conduct yourself on

the track! I pimped you better than that."

Whore: "What had happed was that he started flashing money

in my face and he wouldn't leave us alone."

Mack: "If any of you bitches want to be with Shorty then pack

your shit up right now and roll with Shorty! As a matter of fact

get your mother fucking asses up right the fuck now and get my

mother fucking money right!"

The Meeting

47

Shorty: "Didn't I pay yawl mother fuckers yesterday?

Police: "Yes you did Shorty."

Shorty: "How come one of my bitches got knocked this morning?"

Officer: "The cops that shook your girl down was on another

shift. And I told you that they wanted their cut too!"

Shorty: "I gave yawl mother fuckers $25,000! You better make

that shit work. You were supposed to spread that monetary love

around so I don't have these problems anymore."

Police: "Spread it out?"

Shorty: "Like butter on bread mother fucker!"

Officer: "I'm sorry man. We can't do it like that."

Shorty: "You can't or you won't mother fucker?"

Police: "It just doesn't work like that."

Shorty: "You mother fuckers are supposed to be above the law.

I run the streets and yawl run defense. Play yawl mother fucking

position. Especially if I'm paying for protection! Because if I go

down yawl mother fuckers are going down with me."

Officer: "You know what? You need to play your mother fucking position! And take care of Mack!"

Shorty: "You got me fucked up! Yawl is the mother fucking police. Take that mother fucker down! My job is to pimp hoes and make the money that I'm putting in your pockets!"

Police: "That mother fucking gorilla pimp is out of control!"

Shorty: "People die every damn day. Make something happen!"

Officer: "Unfortunately it isn't that easy! He got some information on us trying to run a train on one of his girls in an alley. So, we have to play it real smooth for a while."

Shorty: "Yawl dumb mother fuckers can't afford a motel room?

Yawl mother fuckers got badges and guns but where the fuck

was yawl mother fuckers at when they were passing out brains?"

Police: "Listen here mother fucker! I was working these streets

before your pimping ass even knew pussy could make money!

So, if think you can take me down let's see who is the last man

left standing when all the gun smoke clears!"

Snitches Get Stitches

Pimp: "Why ain't you been answering your phone pimping?"

Mack: "Because every time that I have been answering that

mother fucker it's always one of my hoes that's on some

bullshit! I done already told the bitch and if I have to pull

up on the bitch I'm definitely putting my foot in her ass! "

Pimp Partner: "I want to get down like you do and put one or

two bitches on the block to get my money up. I just don't know

how to put them bitches in check. What am I supposed to do?"

Mack: "You need some of this good game. Don't give that bitch and inch or she is going to want a mile. And if the bitch talks out turn then you better smack the taste out of that bitches' mouth!"

Pimp Partner: "I can dig it. I'm about to tighten up and learn really quick. I been watching yawl do your thing and when I grow up I want to be a pimp too!"

Shorty: Go ahead and finish the jokes. Don't stop on my account.

Pimp Partner: "I'm just sharing some love with the homies on the block. But you're the only joke around here. We were just talking about you."

Shorty: "Why don't you share that information with me since I'm the topic of conversation? I saw you out here with that 400 pound bitch calling yourself trying to pimp her!"

Pimp Partner: "That's kind of funny Shorty because everybody out here knows that I only have one bitch and that's your mama!"

Shorty: "My mother doesn't look like that bitch. But since you got jokes I'm going to slide your mama out of the nursing home without her false teeth and put that bitch to work!"

Pimp Partner: "I was going to go easy on you but now I'm going to take one of your hoes for that comment."

Shorty: "Which one of my hoes would be stupid enough to

choose a lame ass mother fucking want to be pimp over me?"

Pimp Partner: "Your stupid ass mama. I'm already fucking the

bitch and she can suck a tennis ball through a straw!"

<Shorty pimp smacks him so hard that he falls to the ground.>

Shorty: "My mother is dead you bitch ass want to be pimp!"

Mack: "You can roll up off my block with all that bullshit!"

Shorty: "I was waiting for your bitch ass to say something!"

Mack: "Something! Mother Fucker!"

<Shorty pulls out a gun on Mack and cocks the pistol.>

<Mack pulls out his pistol on Shorty.>

Mack: "You better slow your motherfucking roll or you are

going to go see your bitch ass mother sooner than you think!"

Shorty: "I thought pimping was a non-contact sport?

Can we talk pimp to pimp, player to player? This track ain't that

mother fucking big so we have to learn to come to some kind of

agreement. And you think I'm old and washed up. But we should

be able to find a way to work together and both get this money."

Mack: "Like the money that you are paying the police?"

Shorty: "It's the cost of doing business in this game. You young

ass mother fuckers just don't get it. You have to grease the wheel

if you don't want to hear it squeal like a pig."

Mack: "I'm not running around with the mother fucking police!"

Shorty: "I keep hearing about you hitting licks in the streets.

Sooner or later, they are going to catch up with your ass and you

are going to end up in between a rock and a hard place. And

you're going to wish that you listened to a pimp!"

Mack: "The cold thing about it is that as soon as you no longer

serve a purpose to them those pigs are going to turn their backs

on your pimping ass! I'm about to put you up on this pimping!

What you need to do is get all your raggedy ass bitches together

and take them bitches down the block. This is my mother fucking

stroll but if you show me some respect you can exist here."

Shorty: "Everybody needs somebody and you're going to need a

pimp like me sooner than later! I have some appointments to

keep but think about what I said."

Mack: "If you keep fucking with me then your funeral is going to

be the last mother fucking appointment that you are going to

have to worry about keeping!"

Protect and Serve

Shorty: "This mother fucker Mack thinks that he is god!"

Police: "What should we do about him?"

Shorty: "We are going to put a mother fucking case on his ass!"

Police: Whatever you do make it clean. We don't need any heat!

Shorty: "I want this mother fucker under the jail! You know the

play mother fucker! Don't act like we ain't never done anything

like this before!"

The Big Payback

<Shorty is on the phone with the police.>

Shorty: "I'm putting this thing together as we speak. Give me

about an hour or so and I'll call you back. Jenny come here!

You heard what the fuck I said bitch! Bring your mother fucking

ass over here right the fuck now! I'm not playing with you bitch!"

Jenny: "Here I come daddy!"

Shorty: "Get your narrow ass on in this car and take those heels

off in my shit. Where is my money at bitch? I need my money!

Don't be acting brand new bitch! You break bread when your ass

hits these leather seats! Money first then your bitch ass can talk!"

Jenny: "I got your money right here daddy! I have been working

my ass for you tonight and I was about to catch another trick

when you rolled up on me."

Shorty: "That's good bitch! Stand up on all ten toes when it

comes to getting my mother fucking money like a good bitch!"

Jenny: "I'm all the way down for you daddy. I like the way it

makes me feel when I peel off a nice roll of money for you!"

Shorty: "I feel like a brand-new man when that stack of bread

hits my hand. I was born to Mack and I'll be doing it until the

day that I die. All I have to do now is get that that wet behind

the ears play pimp Mack out of the way and this whole

stroll will be mine again. I tried to hip that simple ass mother

fucker to the game but that mother fucker is smelling himself.

He is walking around with his head up his ass instead of putting

the game to work like a real mother fucking pimp like me."

Jenny: "I heard he had some good game from a few of his

bitches. They tried to get me to choose him. But you're my

daddy and that young mother fucker is working his hoes hard

as fuck. If they don't bring him in $1000 every night he puts

his foot in their ass really good!"

Mack: "Why the fuck are you even talking right now? And why the fuck are you listening to his bitches? I sent you out there to get my mother fucking money and you're out here running your mouth and listening to street gossip! I need to be putting my foot in your funky ass right now but I have bigger and better plans for you my dear."

Jenny: "Thanks daddy! My ass is already sore from fucking these tricks. And I'll be a good bitch and speak when I'm spoken to next time! I was just excited and my pussy was getting wet from giving you all that money."

Shorty: "You better act right bitch or I'll pimp smack you!"

Jenny: "You're turning me on daddy. I need to be smacked

sometimes and you know how to do it just right every time!

Do you want something special tonight?"

Shorty: "As a matter of fact I do bitch!

<Shorty starts beating her and chocking Jenny out.>

Shorty: "Now go tell Mack that I tried to kill you and that's why

you left me and that you are choosing him to be your man! Tell

him that he is the only pimp that isn't scared to come see me and

that's why you are choosing to be with him. And you better make

him believe that shit too or it's going to go really bad for you. Give him this money you just gave me and tell him that you have one

more big money trick tonight. And if you fuck this up, I'm going to

finish what I started with you!"

Jenny: "I won't fuck it up daddy!"

<Meanwhile back on the hoe stroll…The police pull up on one of

Mack's bitches and almost runs her over in the police cruiser.>

Whore: "Don't you blind mother fuckers see a classy bitch trying

to cross the street? You gentlemen have no class at all!"

Police: "Your bitch ass is jaywalking! Get in the car now!"

Whore: "Here you mother fuckers go again with your police

bullshit! All you pigs want is some free pussy! And my pussy

is not for sale when it comes to porky ass pigs!"

<The two police officers grab her and put her in back of their

police car and pull off.>

Whore: "You mother fuckers are tripping! Where the fuck are we

taking me anyways? The police station is the other way!"

Officer: "Bitch shut the fuck up right now! You are in police

custody! If you don't be quiet right the fuck now, I'll put

something in your mouth to do it for you!"

Whore: "You mother fucker are on some straight up bullshit!

Ain't no free pussy around here! Mack is going to be in your

ass again for fucking with me!"

Police: "Shut the fuck up bitch!"

Whore: "Fuck you!"

<Mack gets a knock at his door and grabs his pistol.>

Mack: "What the fuck do you want bitch?"

Jenny: "Shorty just tried to kill me and I don't have anywhere

else to go! I have some money for you and I'll have some more

coming tonight."

Mack: "How much do you have for me bitch?"

Jenny: "$1500!"

Mack: "Come on in out of the cold bitch! I'll take care of you!"

<Jenny hands him the money.>

Jenny: "I'll have some more money for you later."

Mack: "Bitch I heard you twice the first time. How much more

money are you going to have for a pimp?"

Jenny: "$1000!"

Mack: "Bitch you must have some bomb ass pussy!"

Jenny: "It's all yours now daddy!"

Mack: "How are you going to make that money bitch? I can't

even look at you right now! You must have one of those Captain

Save A Hoe mother fuckers who want to rescue a bitch from this

life and live happily ever after mother fuckers!"

Jenny: "I'll clean myself up really good and put on some make up."

Mack: "Well it sounds good bitch!

Are you ready to make a pimp some money?"

Jenny: "I'm ready daddy!"

Mack:" Ok. Get yourself together. I'll have some new clothes for

you to make you feel better and sexy. The rest is up to you bitch.

Now get pretty for that trick so you can get my mother fucking

money right."

Jenny: "OK daddy!"

<Mack leaves her alone and goes back to his other bitches.>

Mack: "Watch that bitch. I don't trust her."

Another whore: "I don't trust that friendly bitch either! I'm on

that bitch like white on mother fucking rice!"

<Jenny gets a phone call from Shorty.>

Shorty: "Where you at bitch? Get your ass back over here!"

Jenny: "I'm on my way right now Sugar Daddy!"

<Shorty gets a knock at his door.>

Shorty: "Who the fuck is it?"

Jenny: "It's me daddy!"

Shorty: "Stop being so mother fucking dramatic and sit your ass

down somewhere. Take this knife over to Mack's and putting it

somewhere that it can be found. And don't get your fingerprints

on it or you are going down for murder."

Jenny: "What about the money I'm supposed to bring him?"

Shorty: "Money? Now you are talking to me like I'm a mother

fucking trick or something! If you do what the fuck I just told

your ass to do you won't need any fucking money! Now get the

fuck out of here and follow my instructions like a good bitch!"

<Mack is speaking with his pimp partner.>

Pimp Partner: "If this drug deal goes down the way that it is

supposed to neither one of us is ever going to have to worry

about money ever again in life."

Mack: "We just have to keep the cops out of our business."

Pimp Partner: "Don't worry about them right now because I just paid off those vice cops that lock people up for bullshit drug cases. And as long as the money keeps flowing both ways then we won't have any legal problems."

Mack: "We are going to have to take Shorty out of the game because he has a fucking hard on for me and my bitches!"

Pimp Partner: "We need to squash that beef with Shorty and worry about making money off these mother fucking streets! That situation is only going to lead to death or jail. You know he has those crooked cops watching your every move."

Mack: "I don't give a fuck about those pigs!"

Pimp Partner: "You know how game is Mack. You have to give a fuck because your life is always on the line in these streets. And a mother fucker close to you can turn on you like a door knob at a moment's notice. He is going to try to get somebody close to you to set you up. You have to get your priorities straight and keep your mind focused on making this bread."

Mack: "Right now my mind is focused on putting Shorty in a wooden box 6 feet under. I know his ass is coming for me so I have to stay ready at all mother fucking times."

<The police roll up on Mack when he gets into his car.>

Officer: "Where is your partner at?"

Mack: "Fuck you, you, and especially fuck you!"

Officer: "Get the fuck out of the car right the fuck now!"

Mack: "For what? I haven't broken any laws today!"

Officer: "You're going to jail mother fucker!"

Police: "Check the car for evidence!

<Mack and his Pimp Partner gets arrested and taken in for

questioning.>

Detective: "I have a few questions about a woman named

Kimberley Jackson that you have been known to associate with."

Mack: "What about that her? The last time I seen that bitch she

was paying me some money that she owed me!"

Detective: "Have you had disagreements or altercations with

Misses Kimberly Jackson lately?"

Pimp Partner: "I have been known to have a few with my wife.

And I don't pay much attention to any other bitches in the

streets. But that name doesn't really ring a bell."

Detective: "You're a sleazy ass pimp Mack!"

Mack: "Pimp or husband? Because all of that is the same shit to

me. I take care of my bitches and my bitches take care of me.

You can put whatever title you want on it playboy."

Detective: "If I ever had a problem with my wife, we would get a

divorce. All I keep hearing about your pimping ass is that you

beat the shit out of your bitches and take all of their money."

Pimp Partner: "This is bullshit! You have nothing on me pig.

Why the fuck did you bring me in for questioning? Because I need

to let my lawyer know as soon as mother fucking possible!"

Mack: "So what the fuck are you going to do? Are you going to

 arrest me? I already know this is bullshit and you don't have a

single shred of evidence against me. It's your call playboy

because I need to make a phone call if I happen to need some

bail money."

Pimp Partner: "Arrest me. Read me my rights. Do something.

Make this shit make sense to me and my homeboy. We are

sitting down here like crash test dummies in your pig pen."

Mack: "We both have better things to do mother fucker!"

Pimp Partner: "You're supposed to be a detective so get on your

mother fucking job and start detecting shit! You limp dick lame

ass mother fucker! I got shit to do in these streets."

Detective: "Well this is what is about to happen right the fuck

now! I'm going to take you down the hallway then your little

pretty pimping asses are going to walking into this line up. Now

get your pimping asses up and follow me!"

Pimp Partner: "You know I'm getting a little bit tired of your funky attitude. and I don't appreciate it at all. If you keep fucking with me trust and believe me you are going to lose your job mother fucker!"

Detective: "Mack let's go mother fucker! You stay the fuck here!"

<The detective takes Mack to the police lineup room.>

Inmate: "What they got you in for jack?"

Pimp Partner: "All I know is that I need to make a phone call."

Inmate: "I got a burner in here you can use it."

Pimp Partner: "Thanks bro I owe you a favor."

Inmate: "Just put some money on my books."

<Pimp Partner makes a phone call.>

Pimp Partner: "Don't ask any questions. Just listen. Email one

of those pictures down to the Detectives Division right now."

<Pimp Partner makes another call to the mayor's office.>

"Let me advise you to listen to me and not say a fucking word

right now, otherwise your smiling face is going to be on the front

page of the early edition newspaper. "

The Mayor: "Who the fuck is this?"

Pimp Partner: "I told you to shut the fuck up listen. Check your

email inbox! I just sent you a message!"

The Mayor: "What the fuck is this a joke?"

Pimp Partner: "This isn't a fucking joke! Check your messages!"

The Mayor: "Ok. I see. What do you want from me money?"

Pimp Partner: "We can talk about that shit later. Right now, me and my partner Mack need to be released from police custody immediately because your punk ass police officers are trying to put a case on us. And don't try no funny shit or get any bright ideas because I have a lot more pictures of you in compromising positions."

The Mayor: "Understood sir. That is not a problem and I will make it happen as soon as I get off the phone with you. I'm going to need some addition information so I can expedite the process."

Pimp Partner: "Ok anything you need I got you."

The Mayor: "Got it sir. Not a problem."

<The Police snatch Jenny off of the stroll and take her in.>

Police: "Me and mother fucking Mrs. Jones. Who did that pimp do

to your fucking face? Who fucked up your beautiful face Mrs.

Jones? You have such a pretty face. It's a fucking shame that

somebody had the audacity to fuck it up the way that they did.

Can I look inside of your purse? What the fuck do we have here

Mrs. Jones? Don't tell me this is what I think it is?"

<The police find the knife that she was supposed to plant on

Mack. Now she has some explaining to do about the evidence.>

Jenny: "I want to talk to my lawyer right the fuck now!"

Police: "You don't have a fucking lawyer!"

Jenny: "I know my fucking rights! Fuck you mother fucker!"

Police: "No Fuck you! You don't fucking have any rights and

you don't have a fucking lawyer. We got your bitch ass! We

are about to give this knife to our forensics team and see what

they have to say about it bitch! Your ass is fucking grass! You

are going down for the murder of Kimberly Jackson!"

Jenny: "What the fuck happened to her?"

Police: "I'm going to let you sit here and marinate and think hard about your next move because your next move is always your best move. This is a life-or-death situation. And you are going to have to figure out how you are going to get out from under of this murder case?"

Jenny: "What happened to Kimberly? And why the fuck are you keeping me in this room? I'm not under arrest! I know my fucking rights!"

Pimp Partner: "Let's make a toast to our incredibly photogenic mayor of the city. It's a mother fucking chess game and we are about to checkmate these mother fuckers! Now that we have the mayor in our back pocket we are practically untouchable!"

Mack: "That was a cold move we pulled off today to get his crooked ass on our team and it didn't cost us a dime."

Pimp Partner: "And with other crooked cops out the way we can gone ahead and get at Shorty. His ass is right there for the taking. His queen is occupied and the king is exposed. It's time try to put him out of the game and take over this whole street kingdom."

Mack: "I don't give a fuck about Shorty! But with him dead or

alive his bitches have to work and they are about to be working

form my team if they want to eat out here on these streets."

Pimp Partner: "I don't know about you but I'm sick and tired of

jumping in and out of alleys trying to duck and dodge the police.

We should get a key to the city because we have revolutionized

the pimping game. We own the fucking police and the streets."

Mack: "I would like to toast to the revolution of the institution

of prostitution. We are taking the game to another level. I'm

taking these bitches from the ghetto streets to the executive

suites. I like the way we are pursuing this shit to create an

entrepreneurship right here in the hood."

<Mack is on the corner politicking with some other pimps.>

Old school pimp: "Mack let me tell you something about the

old days. I was so serious about this pimping. I was so serious

with my first hoe that I told her that I was a pimp and the bitch

said, "For real?" and I didn't know the first thing about pimping.

But I was so serious about it that me and that bitch caught the

bus down to the track to get my money. Then I got a transfer to

get us back to where we came from. That's the day that I fell

in love with this pimping game."

Mack: "That's some real pimping if I don't say so myself."

Old school pimp: "This mother fucking pimp shit is magic. I broke the richest bitch in this whole mother fucking world. I was on top of the hill like God. Now it's your turn Mack. It's your mother fucking turn partner."

Shorty: "What's up pimps and hustlers? I know all of yawl is going to the upcoming players ball where they are going to crown me king of the mother fucking streets!"

Young pimping: "I know you're up for the crown big pimping!"

Shorty: "No mother fucking doubt. I'm going to win it all!"

Old school pimp: "Look at that hater Shorty. That mother fucker

wishes that he was pimping like you Mack!"

Shorty: "So what have you been up to pimping?"

Young pimping: "You know I'm just out here try to get my money

and keep things rolling in the right fucking direction which is in

my mother fucking pockets!"

Shorty: "I'll see you around young player. Keep it pimping!"

Young pimping: "Ok player partner see you at the players ball!"

<Shorty walks up on a group of young ladies.>

Shorty: "Are you young ladies cold? My pimping can definitely

keep you warm and safe. I'll be your Prince Charming!"

Mack: "Look at that weak ass pimping. Those broke bitches ain't

about getting that paper any mother fucking ways. I can see way

from over here that those bitches aren't about this life."

Shorty: "The player's ball is tonight. You pretty young ladies

should come with me my as my V.I.P guests. I'm not about these

punk ass bitches out here. I only associate with the finest

females on the planet and I attract them with my cold ass

game. All you have to do is follow because I can lead you

to the promised land. All you have to do is follow a few simple

rules. No reckless eyeballing. And keep your attention on me

at all mother fucking times. And you will see and touch more

money than you ever have in your entire lives. With your much

needed assistance we can make all of our wildest fantasies

become a reality. I'll dress you in the finest garments and lead

you around in the luxury of exotic automobiles. All the other

women will envy you and want to be in your place."

Pimp Partner: "What's up Mack daddy?"

Mack: "Always pimping you dig. What's going on with you?"

Pimp Partner: "Still maintaining out here."

Shorty: "You sure are looking good today but I know for a fact

that you can do better. If I can make you smile maybe you will

stay awhile with me. My name is Shorty by the way. So what do

you do for a living?"

Young lady: "I'm a real estate broker."

Shorty: "Well I definitely need a place to lay my head down.

And I want to support your dreams and help you make them

a reality!"

Young lady: "Well here is one of my business cards. Keep in

contact with me and let me know when you're ready to make

a move in another direction."

Pimp Partner: "I see you out here looking all good and fly doing

your thing out here on the track trying to catch some honey. I

see you balling like a boss player doing it big and everything."

Mack: "You know how the fuck I do it pimping!"

Shorty: "I'm definitely going to reach out and touch you very

soon in the near future. I like your attitude and your vision."

Young lady: Ok Shorty. I'm looking forward to hearing from you.

Mack: "Look at this sucker. He is not to be trusted. Trust and

believe that he isn't a mother fucking real pimp. Shorty is a

straight up long headed hating mother fucking sucker!"

Pimp Partner: "Look I told you already if you want me to lay this

mother fucker down just let me know and I got you."

Mack: "Don't even trip pimping. That's for me to do. Right now

I'm going to kill him and leave him breathing. I'm going to fade

his ass and make him a memory on these streets."

Pimp Partner: "Mack, don't let this affect our business. We have

come way too mother fucking far to fall off now."

Mack: "Pimp I got this. It's nothing."

< One of Shorty's whores gets into his car.>

Whore: "What the fuck is going on with you? You got me

selling ass out here on the track and you're out here talking to

square bitches!"

< Shorty pimp smacks her back to reality. >

Shorty: "What the fuck is wrong with you bitch! I done told your

ass to stay the fuck out of grown folks' business. I'm a mother

fucking pimp and you know how I do this shit. I was exercising

my mother fucking game and seeing if I can pull one of those

fine young bitches in my direction. Next time I'm gone send

your mother fucking ass to pull the bitch for me and I don't give a fuck if you have to eat the bitch's pussy and asshole,

you better bring that bitch back to me. And don't be putting

no mother fucking bass in your voice when you talk to a pimp!

You better be lucky that I didn't put my entire foot in your

funky ass! No get your out back out there and get my mother

fucking money. I want double the money for your ass talking

out of turn and getting out of pocket!"

Whore: "I'm sorry daddy for talking out of turn and disrespecting

the game. I'll eat as much pussy and ass as you want me to. And

I'll bring that bitch back to you with a bankroll in her hand."

Shorty: "I don't know what's spinning around in your head,

but I do all the thinking for you and you better get some act

right before I have to put your bitch ass in place. And what you

need to be thinking about is how you are going to double my

money with your tricks. That mouth and pussy is going to be

working twice as hard bitch. Now get your funky ass out of my

car and go get my mother fucking money bitch!"

Whore: "Ok daddy. I'll stay in a bitch's place. And the next time

that you see me I'll be making it rain and putting twice as much

money in your pockets for me fucking up!"

<The night of the player's ball.....>

Player Pimp: "It ain't no game if it ain't good game. And you're

a mother fucking lame if not blessed by this mother fucking

pimping game. And you bring shame to this game if you can't

even maintain. Tell her to go other there to use that honey to get

that money. And my bread better be right and always on time."

Whore: "You are going to kill them tonight daddy! You are

looking so good that I wish I still had my virginity that I could

be giving it up to you if even if I had to go in my pockets to get

that big daddy dick."

Mack: "When I walk into the room tonight all eyes are going to be on me even the men are going to be eyeballing me like a mother fucker. And I guarantee some of these so-called pimps are going to be losing some hoes tonight because they will be choosing and begging to be with a real mother fucking boss player. I just feel sorry for the haters because they are going to be working overtime if they want to keep up with all this pimping. They are going to be blinded at what they see like they are looking into the sun. Nobody can deny my pimping and my style is so unique that it can attract the coldest freaks. They better watch and study this game so they don't miss a fucking thing.

<Mack is getting ready for the player's ball.>

Mack: "When I walk into the room it's like I'm barefoot on ice.

Mother fuckers is gone shiver because I'm dressed so nice. And

bitches are blinded by what they see. It's like they are staring

straight at their guiding light. And any bitch on the stroll will

tell you that Mack is the one! I revolutionized this pimp shit! And

any mother fucker that is pimping has studied under me. And if

he gets out of line we are going to get in some gangster shit. And

he damn well better be ready to see me because that hating

mother fucker could never in a million fucking years be me!"

<At the player's ball…. Lights, camera, action…>

Triple OG: "Do you have anything to say to your fans before

you blow this whole thing away with your pimping?"

Mack: "As long as there is a track you best better believe that I'm

going to be the #1 Mack! Now let me go get this mother fucking

trophy for player of the year. My audience awaits. These hoes are

going to be falling to the floor choosing a real mother fucking

pimping ass player tonight!"

Triple OG: "Just as you said it, it shall be done big pimping!"

<Mack enters the player's ball with the confidence of a pimp.>

Triple OG: "What's up pimping?"

Pimpology: "Well you know the only thing going up is the cost

of living and the price of pussy! And my main man Mack is going

to walk away with this trophy. We are here to celebrate him and

his achievements in this game. And these weak as pimps are

going to be walking away limping!"

Ole school pimping: "We came here to show Mack love and to

see him win that crown. It's going down tonight!"

Good Game: "I'm here representing my young pimp partner

Mack. He deserves this trophy more than anybody. These lames

and squares are already drooling at the mouth waiting to hate

on him. I can see it in their eyes because they are lacking the

game to make it to the next level of pimping and pandering!

It is the lifestyle that we lead as men of leisure!"

Young pimp: "Come here baby. You need to get with some of

of this expensive ass mother fucking pimping before I change

my mind and leave you here wondering what your life could

have been like with a real mother fucking pimp in your life!"

Whore: "Well I already have a man and he is showing me big

things already. And that mother fucker keeps my pussy and

my mind dripping with anticipation!"

Young pimp: "Is that right now? You need to get with a real

mother fucking player that is going to raise your money and

status up to the next level!"

Whore: "Well all that sounds good to me big pimping."

Young pimp: "It sounds good because it is good. I don't just want to benefit from our arrangement. I want both of us looking and dressing good out on here these streets. I want the tricks to lose their minds when they see the finest bitch that God himself has blessed them to see while you're out here representing me."

Whore: "So what do you want me to do about me and you making a connection? And how soon can we make it happen daddy?"

Young pimp: "Well you better start choosing before I walk away and find a better bitch to share my dreams with! And before I do I want to ask you a few questions. Can you buy me a house?"

Whore: "Yes I can daddy!"

Young pimp: "Can you buy me expensive rims for my car?"

Whore: "Yes daddy!"

Young pimp: "Can you fly across the world and visit exotic places

with me as we wine and dine with the rich and famous?"

Whore: "Of course daddy!"

Young pimp: "Then I need to be fucking with you bitch!"

Whore: "You got my pussy all wet think about our future

together. And I'm so motivated to get this money for you!

I'm going to fuck you good and put all of my money in your

pockets. You haven't seen a money-making machine like me

in action. I'll break my trick's pockets for everything they have."

Young pimp: "Get on that pole and twerk for me! Show me

what your fine ass is working with. Make me feel like a king!"

Triple OG: "I have never called a man gorgeous ever in my life.

But what is happening with you 'Gorgeous One'?"

Gorgeous One: "I'm ready for the festivities that are going on

tonight, and I'm trying to pull me some new thoroughbreds for

my stable because I'm the 'Gorgeous One' and the bitches know

that I am able to rock their world without a cable. I will jump

start a bitch and have her out there turning more tricks than an

ATM machine. I'll put a bitch on the block and give her a quota and she better have all of my money on time!"

Triple OG: "I can't stand a bitch with excuses. Never let a

bitch pimp you and tell you any mother fucking thing! Look

at that bitch dead in the eyes and make her tell you what you

want to hear. Then you tell the bitch your expectations and

the consequences of not meeting them. Then that bitch will know

that you are 100 percent serious about getting your money or

the next move is a foot in her funky ass!"

Old school: "This is so fucking beautiful. And the real beauty is

controlling your bitches because when it comes to getting my

money they know what time it is and they know that it's all on a bitch to make this thing happen!"

Triple OG: "It's time to acknowledge the man of the hour!

Shorty what's going on with your pimping ass?"

Shorty: "It's all good pimping. My game is taking over!"

Triple OG: "Well let me ask you something pimping. When

you come to an even like the player's ball do you already

know whether you are the big winner or not?"

Shorty: "Well the way I see it player. When they invented this

award and came up with the concept of it there is no doubt

that it's all about a cold pimping ass player like myself. So, let

the chips fall where they may which I predict is right here in my mother fucking pockets like always!"

Triple OG: "I know a pimp is supposed to be clean but damn!

You are definitely here representing the game!"

Slick Ricky: "This is that New York shit! These young ass pimps

don't know nothing about style. You have to dazzle a bitch and

look good from your head to the floor. Make that bitch wonder

what it would be to experience being with a man like me. You

have to motivate that bitch to make the impossible a reality.

That's that real mother fucking pimping! You have to be able

to do what you want and have what you want at the same damn

time. I love this mother fucking game!"

Triple OG: "That's right pimping! And the game loves you!"

Slick Ricky: "The game must be good to you too player.

I see you making it happen from long distance reaching out

and putting a bitch in line and definitely in the right direction

to get that paper connection consistently."

Triple OG: "I see you Good Game. Tell me something good!"

Good Game: "Ain't not game if it isn't good game. The way I

move these lames try to imitate. But then I make new moves

and innovate. Now they are confused and slow to the real

concepts of the game. Those are the ones that we label the

original player haters because they will never understand the concept of the game. They will never understand the rules of

the game. And they will never be able to play the game the way

that it was meant to be played. They just watch us real pimps

play it and sit around trying to figure it out. It is simple and plain.

You are either born a pimp or you are born a lame. And the

sooner that you accept your place in life then the sooner you will

make things happen on your level. Stop watching us and start

making real mother fucking moves out here square ass haters."

Triple OG: "That's definitely some good game for the haters!"

Good Game: "It ain't nothing but love for this game. I'm still

down and I'm waiting to see if Mack or Shorty wins the crown!"

Triple OG: "It's an international thing for me. It's all love. And

I encourage my bitches to spread love all over the world! And I

get all the love from my bitches in return!"

DC Pimp: "Everything I do is federal, even my pimping game!"

DC Whore: "You got that right daddy!"

DC Pimp: "I'm going to pimp until I do what?"

DC Whore: "Until you die baby!"

DC Pimp: "Are you going to ride?"

DC Whore: "Yes I'm going to ride for you daddy!"

DC Pimp: "How long are you going to ride?"

DC Whore: "I'm going to ride until I die daddy!"

DC Pimp: "Are you going to ride with me all the way?"

DC Whore: "I'm going to ride with you all the way daddy!"

<Mack and Shorty meet at the player's ball.>

Shorty: "You know you owe me a bitch, right?"

Mack: "You're the mother fucking playing street games trying to

put a case on me. And now that you done fucked up then you

want me to be held responsible for your mother fucking actions."

Shorty: "That was my top money-making bitch and I gambled

on her life for yours. You know like trading places but somehow

you got out of the life in prison trap that I set for you!"

Mack: "I see you out here trying to checkmate a pimp. But you

forgot that I know how to play this game too. And I play to win

so sooner or later I'll be at your throat like a pit bull gone wild!"

Shorty: "Thank goodness that you don't hold grudges. I was

starting to think that you were going to retaliate for my

indiscretions. My girl Jenny Jones was a pawn in this

game but since I had to sacrifice her then I want one of your

bitches in return!"

Mack: "You done lost your rabbit ass mind if you think that's

going to actually happen. You sliced a bitch up and tried to

plant evidence on a player. Just like the fuck you said you

sacrificed your bitch and didn't get me caught up in your trap.

Word on the street your girl Jenny got caught with the evidence

so, you lost another bitch hating on me. That goes against the

rules of the game and now you have to suffer the consequences.

So, what you need to do right now is change mother fucking

directions at the next intersection and slide on out while you're

still breathing. That trying to put a mother fucking case on me

was definitely a bad idea. You thought that you could just set a player up for a life sentence and inherit my bitches by default.

But I was one step ahead of you in the game and you're the one

taking losses by putting your bitches on a head on collision with

danger. Get your mother fucking mind right before it ends up

in little pieces when I blow it out all over the fucking concrete!"

Shorty: "Is that a threat mother fucker?"

Mack: "It's more like a promise. And the more bullshit you stay on

the quicker I'm going to creep up on your bitch ass! I make

promises and not excuses like you and your bitches!"

Shorty: "I don't want all your hoes. I just want your bottom

bitch that put you in this game. I heard that bitch's pussy is the

best on the stroll. Then we can call it even and we both can do

our thing without getting in each other's way again. I'll even be

willing to give you a pass!"

Mack: "She would rather work for me butt ass naked in below

zero weather than choose to be with a lame ass pimp like you!

Because you are a simple-minded mother fucker who will never

make it to the big time like me. I'm ten steps ahead of a mother

fucker like you. And while you're sitting here trying to distract a

pimp with all this small talk, what you need to do is put your cape on and play captain save a hoe because right the fuck now

my bitches got your bitches hemmed up in the bathroom and in

mother fucking minute you're about to be hoe less and broke."

Shorty: "Yea alright mother fucker!"

<Shorty goes running to the lady's room.>

Mack: "Get your best bottle of champagne ready! I'll be right

back to celebrate my victory over this want to be pimp!"

<One of Mack's whores has a knife to the neck ok of one of

Shorty's whores as the drama unfolds in the women's

restroom.>

Mack's whore: "She is about to be a dead bitch!"

Short's whore: "If this bitch as much as scratches my neck you

better smoke her mother fucking ass!"

<One of Shorty's whores has a pistol on Mack's whore who is

holding it to the neck of Shorty's whore.>

Shorty's whore with the gun: "I'll blow another hole in your ass!"

Mack's whore with the knife: "Bitch ain't nobody scared of you!"

Shorty's whore: "Bitch shut your ass up right now!"

Mack's whore: "She can't shoot everybody. Let's show these

weak ass bitches that we are about that life! Let's rush this bitch!

Mack's other whore: "You punk ass bitch! Why are you pointing

the gun at me? I ain't said two mother fucking words to your

bitch ass! You better be careful hoe!"

Shorty's whore: "Somebody needs to tell this fat bitch to shut the

fuck up before I put a bullet in her ass!"

Mack's other whore: "Who are you calling a fat bitch?"

Shorty's whore: "Bitch you heard me! I didn't stutter!"

Mack's whore: "Yea if you name it, my girl ate it! Her specialty is

eating dicks. My girl is a dick swallowing maniac!"

Shorty's whore: "Yawl all about to be some dead bitches!"

Shorty: "Bitch put that gun down before I smack the shit out

of that pretty little face of yours! All of you bitches are out of

pocket and need a pimp to get your asses back in line and

stay in a bitches place!"

Shorty's bitch: "Ok daddy. But these bitches started this gangster

shit and we had to step up and ride on these messy bitches!"

Mack's whore: "Bitch we were just about to smash the gas on you

funky ass bitches! I'll show you some gangster shit since Shorty

came to save his hoes from this bloody ass massacre!"

Shorty: "Bitch you better respect this pimping! You ain't my

Bitch, but I will put my foot all up in your ass and you will know

what my pimping is all about!"

Mack's whore: "You better back the fuck up before I blast your

mother fucking ass into the middle of next year pimping! Don't

make me fuck you up! I'll turn that plaid suit into polka dots!"

Shorty: "So you're a mother fucking gangster now?"

Mack's whore: "Step to me mother fucker and find out the hard

way! I'll blast your ass and leave you here bleeding like a stuffed

pig! So you better make your next move your best move and

fall the fuck back you want to be ass Mack!"

Mack: "You might want to stand down and put some act right

into your life because my bitches are ready, able, and willing

to put a pimp like you down! You are sharp in that plaid suit

but I don't think you would like how it would look with blood

stained polka dots on it? So, what kind of fashion statement do

you want to make living and breathing or dead-on arrival?"

Shorty: "This shit ain't over Mack! I'll be coming to see you."

Mack: "For sure playboy! You know what time it is. And only a

cold ass mother fucking pimp like me can set a trap for a rat like

you to snap his mother fucking neck. So, you better learn some

mother fucking respect if your bitch ass wants to survive in these streets. I see death around the corner for you if you keep

fucking with my pimping. Now you and your hoes roll out of

this mother fucker because this mother fucker right here is about

to be crowned player of the mother fucking year!"

Shorty's whore: "It ain't over for you bitches either. I'll see your

mother fucking funky asses in the parking lot later!"

Mack's whore: "Whatever bitch!"

Shorty: "What the fuck are you bitches looking so happy for? Get

the fuck out of my face before I fuck you hoes all the way up!"

Triple OG: "Good evening ladies and gentleman, it is now time

to move on to the award ceremony portion of this sacred event.

Before we begin let me tell you how honored I am to be a

member of this illustrious organization of pimps and players!

Because in the beginning if you remember God created the

earth. He then put Adam and Even into the fabulous garden of

Eden. Adam was entrusted with the direction that neither of them

indulged in the forbidden fruit of knowledge. Because Adam was

a square he allowed the bitch Eve to go against what God had

instructed him to do. Since that time there has been a league

of extraordinary gentlemen that have been assigned as the

care takers of the female minds, bodies, and souls. These are

the gentlemen that we call pimps and players. Pimp meaning

that pussy is my priority. These are profession individuals

managing pussy. Possessors of intellectual mind power. Now

without any further interruption it is time for the main event.

I now present the trophy for the upcoming Mack of the Year.

This means that he has been pimping all 365 days of this year

without taking a day off to rest. It is my pleasure to announce

the winner of this much sought-after achievement."

<At the local police department.>

Detective: "Look here Miss Jones. The razor that we found in

your possession matches the weapon that was used in the

murder of Kimberly Jackson. But you already knew that, didn't

you? And it probably has something to do with who ever

pimp smacked the fuck out of your pretty face. So, you better

wise the fuck up real fast because now is the time to step up

and co-operate with this murder investigation. What I really need

to know is how this straight razor blade got to be on your person

and in your purse?"

Jenny: "I honestly don't know how it got there. The only thing

I can do is talk to my lawyer and ask him how it appeared out

of thin air."

Detective: "You got a smart-ass mouth bitch! That may be the

fucking reason that you got your face smacked. I might even

let you see a lawyer if in fact you decide to be a co-operating

witness. But what I really need to know right the fuck now is

where did you get the razor from? "

Jenny: "I'll wait to talk to my attorney because I feel like you

are trying to put words in my mouth because my man has

nothing to do with any murders and neither do I."

Detective: "Ok if that's how you want to play it. You are already an accessory to the crime simply by handling and tampering with evidence in a murder investigation. We don't even have to connect any dots because all roads lead to you. So you can either take all of the weight or lessen your role and have a chance to completely walk away from it as a co-operating witness. The ball is in your court now. And ain't not mother fucking lawyer going to get your sweet ass from up under a life sentence."

<A man enters the investigation room dressed like a lawyer.>

Lawyer: "Hello Misses Jones. My name is….."

Jenny: "I know who the fuck you are and I know this con game.

I don't want to make any fucking deals. The police set me up and

I fucking know it. They planted that fucking razor on me so they

could take my man Shorty down. The police can't stand that

pimping ass mother fucker. But I'm a down ass bitch and he will

be here to take care of me if I take the fall. The first cop beat

the shit out of me and tried to rape me. Then he sent this

detective in here after they planted evidence in my purse. This

is some straight up bullshit. I know my fucking rights. And if I

gave up some pussy I wouldn't even be sitting here right now."

Lawyer: "Who the fuck is Shorty?"

Jenny: "Where the fuck have you been anyways? Are you fucking paying any attention to the words that are coming out of my mother fucking mouth? Anyways Shorty sent me over to Mack's house to plant this fucking razor on him but before I could even get over there to do it some fucking police officers kidnapped me off the streets and tried to fuck the shit out of me. Those nasty ass pigs were probably trying to run a train on me. But since I didn't want to give up any head or pussy now they are trying to frame me for the murder of one of my good friends."

Detective: "Sorry to interrupt you Misses Jones but I came

here to tell you that your lawyer was running a little late. He

should be here whenever the fuck he gets here. I'm sure that

you will be given an attorney after we file these murder charges

on you and your pimp boyfriend Shorty!"

Jenny: "I thought he was my fucking lawyer!"

Detective: "No he was here to give a polygraph test to prove

your innocence. And we won't be needing his services because

you have already confessed to the homicide of the lovely Misses

Kimberly Jackson."

Lawyer: "Do you want any coffee, tea, or a soda pop? I will be

happy to provide you with some refreshments! It's time for you

 to get acquainted with your new accommodations. Miss Jones."

Jenny: "This is some bullshit! You punk ass mother fuckers set

me the fuck so I would snitch on my man Shorty!"

Detective: "You freely talked to an agent of the police after

waiving your right to remain silent. He simply sat down in the

chair that I was just sitting in and you clearly just told my friend

here that you were part of the conspiracy to send Mack to prison

after your Pimp boyfriend Shorty killed Kimberly Jackson. You

then helped or tried to help Shorty plant this murder weapon on his pimp friend Mack. You soul sisters will do anything for these

dirty pimps. Now you're in a jackpot with no way out. If you're

lucky we will let you wear a wire to get him to confess to the

murder of your other close friend and associate Kimberly Jackson.

We have your sweet ass in between a rock and a hard place.

You're definitely going to snitch on your pimp daddy Shorty. It's

just a matter of time. If not, you can rot in prison and eat fishy

pussy for the rest of your natural life. The choice is yours. That

pimp mother fucker will let you rot in prison while he is out here

smacking some new bitches and getting money out of their nasty

whore asses. He already got you into this trap and once we have your funky ass we are not letting you go. You will die in a

fucking jail cell trying to protect a pimp who doesn't give a

flying fuck about your fishy whore ass!"

Jenny: "I'll ride or die for my man. A mother fucking crooked ass

cop like you would never understand the code of the streets and

my loyalty to the pimping game."

Detective: "There will come a day when you wish you would have

snitched on his pimping ass! And you might even want to

consider the possibility of me and my law enforcement friends

running a train on you for a get out of jail free card, but you still

have to give up your dirty ass pimp Shorty!"

Jenny: "Fuck that and fuck you! I'm not fucking and sucking

on no fucking pork chop eating pigs! I'll eat the next bitches

ass before I put a pig's dick in my mouth or pussy! You silly

ass sick son's of bitches! I'll die in this mother fucker and

finger fuck myself to sleep at night. I'll sleep like a new born

baby in this bitch and get all the pussy I will ever need to satisfy

myself! This is just a lesbian sleepover for me. And I'll be getting

more pussy than you ever will Porky the mother fucking pork

chop eating pig!"

Detective: "They all talk shit until that judge hits the mother

fucking gavel then it's a lifetime of tears and regret."

<Meanwhile back at the player's ball…>

Triple OG: "As I look around, I see that there are several

members know that the next award is pimp of the year. And

as I look at their faces it appears as if you are wondering if it

could possibly be you."

Good Game: "Not if you're really pimping like me!"

Triple OG: "Absolutely because if you haven't been pimping then this is an award where you should not be in attendance for. You should think about stepping your game up or finding some new bitches because this award here is just not given to anybody. This is the equivalent of pimps choosing the top mother fucker Mack in the game. This is a man who has gone over and above the call of duty. I think that I can speak for all of us when I say this was an easy choice this year."

Young pimp: "What the fuck are you saying? I know that I won this mother fucker by a landslide. Check it out. I got this mother fucker on lockdown. Nothing or nobody can stop me now! "

Triple OG: "Sit your mother fucking as down somewhere

youngster. You aren't even nominated for this award! This fool

is trying to get some hoes attention for real. I know game when I

see it. And now I shall continue. It's that type of outburst right

there that will get your name taken completely off the ballot!

The reason that we allow it is because it's past this young

mother fucker's bedtime and he is going to turn into a mother

fucking pumpkin when the street lights come on. Those of us

in the profession know that Good Game is the people's champion.

We love this mother fucker like a family member!"

Good Game: "Ain't no mother fucking game, if it ain't good game!"

Triple OG: "Now as I move on. There was only two real

contestants in this competition. And you know that you were not

one of them with that parade of raggedy ass broke bitches that

need attention and wear clothes from the 99 cents store. There

were only two real contestant for player of the year. Ladies and

gentlemen without any further commotion. More legendary than

a Cadillac, and more deadly than crack, the pimp of the year is

that cold as ice mother fucking Mack!"

Shorty: "Fuck that want to be mother fucker! I'm the real pimp

of the year. My game can run circles around his!"

Mack: "That jealous mother fucker over there talking shit needs

to grow the fuck up! He just got his bottom bitch busted! It's a

great honor to win this award. But what it really tells is that I can

turn a lost hoe into a boss hoe. I love this trophy and I represent

the National Pimping Association. And they can start calling me

Mack Jordan because I have been crowned the Most Valuable

Pimp in this game! Real pimps never fall and real Macks stand

tall on all ten toes as we graduate these hoes to the next level"

Pimp Partner: "You did it man! I'm proud of you pimping!"

Shorty: "Get over her bitch! You heard me hoe!"

Whore: "Ok daddy. I was just trying to holler at my people!"

Shorty: "You ain't got no mother fucking people! Let's go bitch!"

Mack's whore: I'll see your mother fucking ass on the track bitch!

Shorty's whore: "Yawl is some scary ass bitches. Yawl didn't even

have my back when that strong ass hoe had me hemmed up!"

Shorty: "All yawl mother fucking bitches can either shut the fuck

up or get the fuck out of my car right now! I'm about to drop

you hoes off at the spot and none of you bitches better not as

much slam my door when you get out of my fucking car!"

<Shorty calls his dirty cop friends.>

Shorty: "What the fuck is going on? And why is this mother

fucker Mack still on the streets? I give you mother fuckers

good money to do my dirty work! You are the dumbest minions

on the whole mother fucking police force! What the fuck is up?

Yawl said that you were going to arrest his ass!"

Police: "We did arrest him and his partner in crime. Jenny never

showed up with the blade and we can't find her ass. Apparently

they got to the mayor and they ended up getting released

without any charges. And now the Chief of Police and the Mayor

on our asses for bringing him in."

Shorty: "I'll tell you what then. I'm going to Plan B."

Police: "What the fuck is Plan B?"

Shorty: "Look here mother fucker, just meet me at the spot

around midnight and be prepared to get into some gangster shit!"

<Shorty gets rolled up on after he tries to drives off.>

Detective: "Freeze mother fucker! Get the fuck out of the car

right now with your hands the fuck up! And then put your hands

behind your back! Handcuff this piece of shit and put him in

the backseat of my car!"

Shorty: "Get your mother fucking hands off of me!"

<The detective is at the station questioning Shorty.>

Detective: "Do you know a Miss Jenny Jones?"

Shorty: "That bitch is my hoe. She doesn't even think unless I

ok it and give her the green light to converse with a trick."

Detective: "Well she is thinking pretty good for herself in a jail

cell. She informed me that you gave her the green light to take

this here razor over to Mack Robinson's house and plant it where

your police friends could find it!"

Shorty: "I know none of my hoes ain't ever told you some

bullshit like that! My bitches know better than to talk about grown

folks business with any member of law enforcement and they do

what they are told when I give them instructions."

Detective: "So you are saying that if you told Jenny Jones to do

something then she probably has done it?"

Shorty: "I'm a business man in this city and I don't know anything

about a bitch doing anything or telling a bitch to do anything?"

Detective: "You're in the pimping business mother fucker!"

Shorty: "This is some mother fucking bullshit and I don't take

kindly to a mother fucker violating my civil rights!"

Detective: "Fuck you and your mother fucking civil rights!"

Shorty: "And fuck you pig. I know my fucking rights. My

lawyer will be down here immediately to bail me the fuck

out of here!"

Detective: "Do you think that when they are talking about our

civil rights that they are talking about uncivilized mother fuckers

like you? You're a pimp and a fucking murderer!"

Shorty: "Either book me or show me the mother fucking door!"

Detective: "You're lucky that I'm even talking to you! I got you

on tape doing all kinds of illegal shit! Fuck you pimp!"

Shorty: "That's some bullshit. Play me the tape then."

Detective: "Play the fucking tape for this pimp!"

Shorty: "What the fuck is next? Am I going to see the wizard?

Are you going to swing the light back and forth? Then slap me

with phone books until I confess. Is that what you're going to

do detective?"

Detective: "That's funny as fuck! Are you making fun of what I

do for a living pimp? Are you teasing me now? Fuck you! And

you have the right to remain silent! You have the right to a

fucking attorney!"

Shorty: "What's the fucking charge Wonder Bread?"

Detective: "You're under arrest for the murder you fucking pimp!"

Shorty: "I didn't kill the bitch! I only slapped her around from

time to time. And the last time I seen her ass, she was still

breathing and putting money in my hand."

Detective: "How about I fucking slap you around pimp?"

Shorty: "You need to be talking to her old pimp Mack!"

Detective: "I'm a homicide detective! I don't give a fuck about

Mack! I give a fuck about you! Are you waiving your rights

mother fucker? Because I know you have information for me!"

Shorty: "Can you cut me a deal?"

Detective: "It's your lucky fucking day! Because Tuesday is cut

a fucking deal with a pimp day! Talk to me. Because the way I'm

looking at it right now you will never see the light of day again!"

Shorty: "I want my mother fucking freedom!"

Detective: "If you co-operate with me, I have the perfect deal for

you. I'll get you 4 years if you wear a wire for me. "

Shorty: "I was thinking 12 months of home confinement. And

all I have to do is wear an ankle bracelet. If we don't have a deal

then I don't have anything else to say."

Detective: "We have a deal my friend! We made a deal with a

fucking low life pimp. This is your lucky fucking day pimp!"

Shorty: "I don't like Mack anyways. His ass needs to go down

because he needs to learn a valuable lesson about this game."

Detective: "We are not talking about Mack. His pimp shit is small

to me. I'm talking about your cop friends that you have been

paying for protection and the murder of Kimberly Jackson. "

Shorty: "I don't know about all that shit man."

Detective: "It's your freedom and your life on the line."

Shorty: "Ok, Fuck the police! They let me get exposed anyways."

<Shorty is at home waiting to set up the crooked ass cops.>

<One of the cops knock at his door.>

Shorty: "What's up partner?"

Police: "Why is it so dark out here tonight?"

Shorty: "My security light blew out and I didn't have time to

get on top of it but I'll get another one tomorrow. Come on in.

We need to find a way to get Mack locked the fuck up and we

really need to set the perfect trap for his player of the year

ass! That mother fucker has it coming and I'm ready to give

it to him raw and uncut like dope! His mother fucking ass is

mine for the taking with no Vaseline!"

Police: "Where is your phone at Shorty? We have been trying to get ahold of you for about 2 hours. We thought Mack had set you up and left you bleeding in an alley."

Shorty: "No but I definitely want to catch his ass slipping! I got into it with his ass at the players ball and its definitely time to jump into some gangster shit. His ass is always out of pocket and I really need to teach that mother fucker some serious life lessons that his ass will never forget. And he is going to wish that he never decided to fuck with this pimp right here."

Police: "Where did you park your car at?"

Shorty: "I had one of my bitches drop me off. She will be back

in a few hours with my money in hand. I taught that bitch well

how to bring my money on time. And here you mother fuckers

show up late with a bunch of excuses when I told yawl mother

fuckers to meet me at midnight at an entirely different location!

So, what did yawl do to get rid of the body because we don't need

the streets talking? And I don't need any of this shit coming back

on me. I don't pay you mother fuckers top dollars for fuck ups!"

Officer: Why the fuck do you all of a sudden start asking us

about where we been at and what the fuck we have been doing?

Shorty: "Yawl mother fuckers already know that I run this mother

fucker and I don't need any loose ends coming back to me

because that's just how I move mother fuckers!"

Police: "Did somebody get to you because it sounds to me like

you're trying to set a trap for us instead of Mack. Do you know

what happens to snitches in prison? If you don't, I'll tell you.

They will fuck you with a broomstick and put a live rat up

your ass to keep you company."

Shorty: "I don't know anything about that but what I do know is what they will do to crooked cops like you in population. It's all fucking bad for a mother fucker like you two. But anyways back to fucking business and tell me what the fuck happened with that bitch Kimberly Jackson bitch while yawl mother fuckers are acting all hyper active and shit."

Officer: "You ain't never asked us any kind of silly rabbit shit like that before Shorty. I'm starting to think that you're an informant working some shit off because your ass is caught up in some straight up bullshit!"

Shorty: "Get your mother fucking mind right. I ain't no fucking snitch or a rat. I been putting in work with you silly goose mother fuckers since day one. Yawl are fucking up our business relationship right now. Somebody is going to have to make this shit right or yawl ain't getting another mother fucking dime from me! I know you cut the bitch up because I gave you the razor so why would I roll on yawl and implicate myself in a homicide?"

Officer: "My fault big homie. We put our careers on the line to fuck with you and we have a lot more to lose than you do."

Police: "We dumped that bitch in an alley behind the liquor

store after we stabbed her. Now that I think about it, we should

have fucked that bitch before we killed her. She could have

went out with a smile on her face."

Shorty: "That bitch had a golden pussy too. And she loved to

fuck and suck. She was a money maker because she loved

getting dicked down. Me and the homies use to run trains on

her all the fucking time. Rest in peace bitch! The streets are

going to miss all that good pussy and head that she has been

providing to the community."

Officer: "My fault for tripping earlier. My nerves got the best of

me and I was feeling some strange vibes when I got here. Wait

a mother fucking minute. This snitching ass mother fucker is

wearing a wire!"

<One of the officers goes for his gun but Shorty wrestles him

for it. Several shots are fired in the process but nobody gets

hit by any bullets. The then cops run outside to retreat but are

met by a barrage of police officers and law enforcement

vehicles. They both drop their weapons and put their hands up.>

Task Force: "It's a mother fucking raid! Put your hands up!"

Detective: "Get the fuck down on the ground!"

Police officer: "Handcuff these dirty mother fuckers!"

<Shorty quietly tries to slip out of the door and run away but he

is met by Mack who puts a gun to his head.>

Shorty: "What the fuck do you want from me mother fucker?"

Mack: "Your life mother fucker!"

<One of Shorty's bitches is waiting for him to escape and she

pulls a gun on Mack. It's time to get into some gangster shit!>

Shorty's bitch: "Put the pistol down before I get to blasting!"

Mack: "Bitch if I get shot, I'm blowing this mother fucker's brains

all over the sidewalk and your bitch ass is next on my hit list!"

Shorty: "Everybody just calm the fuck down! We can all walk

away breathing if everybody just calms the fuck down! Ok!"

<Shorty pulls out a knife and cuts Mack on his leg. Gunshot's ring

out and Mack and Shorty's bitch shoot each other. And Shorty

steps to Mack with the knife.>

Shorty: "I should do your mother fucking ass but I'm a pimp

first! I'm going to give your ass a pass because I'm trying to

get the fuck out of here smooth with no extra bullshit! Everybody

already knows that we have beef and I would be the number

one suspect or I'd leave your ass here bleeding like a stuffed

pig! You owe me your mother fucking life blood! It ain't no

mother fucking fun when the rabbit got the gun is it? I beat

you at your own mother fucking game but best believe if I

get another chance your life is mine. Now get your lame

pimping ass the fuck out of here! So, what is going to be

mother fucker pimp or die?"

Mack: "Pimp!"

Shorty: "That what I thought mother fucker. You must got nine

mother fucking lives because this one was almost over mother

fucker! You're going to live to see another day, Mack!"

Mack: "I'm going to give you this pocket watch my father gave

me. Every time you see it just remember we are going to cross

paths again mother fucker!"

Shorty: "I have a present for you too mother fucker!"

<Shorty slashes Mack across the face with his knife.>

Shorty: "Take that to remember me by. Every time you look in the mirror it will remind you that I'm coming for your mother fucking ass! The next time I see you I'm going to cut your mother fucking throat!"

<Shorty walks away and starts looking at the pocket watch and Mack pulls out a pistol and unloads on Shorty with 6 shots!>

Mack: "You was finally one step ahead of me but it was time to checkmate your mother fucking ass! Your time is over! I'll see in the next life!"

<Mack picks up his pocket watch and walks away leaving Shorty

to slowly bleed to death. As he walks away, he points the pistol

at Shorty one more time.>

Mack: Bang! Bang! Mother fucker! You're dead! Check and mate!

<Shorty takes his final breath and slumps over dead and limp.>

Pussy Will Sell

The nerve of this bitch! A bitch's main purpose is to service a

Mack. Get that pimp his money by laying on her back. Until

the bitch's feet hurt from working the track. I don't care if

the bitch doesn't sleep. Because that pussy is just a piece of meat

and a means to eat. The bitches are paying how they are

weighing. That's how I stay in the game. How they are paying is

from laying. You can't trust a bitch because their thinking is lame.

Because they need a pimp like me to give them the game.

Playing on these bitches is all I know. Breaking in the bitch to get

my dough. These hoes need to know they place because back

talk will only get a bitch a slapped in the face. Those bitches get

sprung on the game I run. Bitch I'm seasoned. If she tells

you that pussy ain't selling then she's lying. That bitch is

tricking you. Bitch be all that you can be. Me and my pimps

are hard as hell. I'll pimp smack a bitch and get her clientele.

And get her a room at a plush hotel. Then I'll send a bitch out

there to get my mail. If she gets slammed, cracked or goes to jail

you don't have to worry because I'm coming through with that

bail. I put you on the track like that for real because you all know

and I know that your pussy will sell.

My bitches have some bomb ass pussy! You want the honey.

I want the money. Wherever I go it's all the same. The pussy

got a name but it might change. Depending on the weather or

her mood that day that cat is going to get scratched if that trick

is going to pay. If you are down with me then work that track.

And don't come back until you get my scratch. And bring it all

to me because I got game and I call it pimpology. The bitch

threw a dollar at me. I threw it back now she is following me.

I put this pimping down 7 days a week.

You say you broke hoe. Bitch listen to me because there are all

kind of tricks that pay for pussy. There goes the corner girl. If

you come back with no money then you're getting pimp smacked

up. I might hit you with the pimp stick. And bitch think twice

before asking for some dick. A pimp like me got paid. And a

hoe like you got played. Now listen to the sounds of the bell ring.

It's cash going on like Ching! Ching! Get up get out and get

something and I see myself sending you on the track to

get it pumping. To let you tell it I'm out here pimping for free.

But that ain't me because I got too much hog in me.

I dog hoes like you for fun. Because that bitch that keeps coming

back is my number one. Pimping ain't easy but it's a whole lot

of fun with me with you and me on the track playing one on. Get

dough in the snow in Idaho. One thing for sure when all fails.

These bitches go get my mail because we all know in rain,

sleet or snow that pussy will sell.

Cautionary Tale

There is one aspect of the game that I haven't covered. Pimping

is glamorized in American society. But as you may well know it is

an illegal act that is now being severely punished. Even though

most women in this game are very willing participants there are

some women who are being trafficked. Every year thousands of

young girls run away from home and without a doubt a certain

percentage of them will run into a pimp who will take them in

with open and loving arms but at some point, most of these

young women will be put in a position in which they will have

to survive on the streets. Some of these girls will turn their first trick either by choice or by force. It is a blatant reality

and a fact of life. There are too many scenarios and situations

to describe. Myself personally I would never force any woman

to do anything against her will but realistically adults make

their own individual decisions and those decisions often result in

consequences. There are definitely legal penalties that one might

have to face if you get caught up by law enforcement. The main

reason I am bringing this up is because I have recently found

myself in a legal situation in which I have been charged with

promoting prostitution which in my case is a 4th degree felony.

I won't discuss the details of my current state of affairs because

my case is still pending. The only thing that I can really say about

the matter is that it involves entrapment and illegally obtained

evidence and I am currently facing a mandatory sentence of

6 to 18 months if I am found guilty. I can also tell you that a

person who is convicted of these same charges on the level of

1st, 2nd or 3rd degree can be also forced to register as a sex

offender because they are accused of either physical force or

intimidation of an alleged victim in which they forced them to

perform sex acts against their will which is basically considered

rape and prostitution because they force a woman to perform

sex acts in exchange for money or something of value. My goal

at this point is to educate you to the subsequent consequences

of your potential actions. It has been stated over and over again

for years that pimping isn't easy. This is why many pimps send

their women out with instructions because if you get caught up

in the legal system they can punish you severely for your alleged

actions with your female participating party member. I am

certainly, fighting my case and I am warning anybody who is

attempting to enter this game to beware of the long hand of the

law. They are making any form of pimping a high crime

punishable up to 11 years or more depending on the entire

aspect of what you are being accused of. I'm not even in the

game at this point in my life. I have moved on to bigger and

better things but at this point it is what it is. And I am currently

being forced to participate in this crooked American justice

system and I have no idea what the outcome will be. All that I

know is that I am aware of the facts in my case and I am fully

aware that there is no actual evidence that either I committed a

crime or my co-defendants committed any actual crime. What I

can say is that the police officers in my case are guilty of

entrapment and are trying their best to manufacture evidence

that doesn't exist.

The game teaches us all a lesson. I have thoroughly been

enjoying my life of leisure writing books and indulging in

several other legitimate business ventures but it may come

to a brief interruption if I am somehow convicted of this alleged

offense. What I can tell you is that this is not the end only a new

beginning. I'm currently waiting to see if the grand jury is going

to bring back an indictment on these charges and I am

thoroughly studying the legal facts and arguments related to

the crime which I am alleged to have committed. One thing I do

know about the legal system is that it is stacked against the

defendant who is supposed to be presumed innocent. And law

enforcement will break all of their own rules in an effort to

convict you whether you are guilty or not. So, keep it pimping

and continue to enjoy all of the books in my pimp game series

as well as all of the other books that I will continue to push out.

Writing is my calling and sooner or later the world will appreciate

my great works of literary art. I have been enjoying this journey.

Look forward to my upcoming new releases that will be coming

in the very near future. I will be releasing a new volume of the

Pimp Chronicles that will include the latest two books in my

Pimp Game series which will be a Platinum Pimps and Players

Edition that will include all the books in my Pimp Game series all in one volume. It is an accomplishment that I am very proud

of as a writer. My goal from the very beginning of this series

was to educate and entertain my readers. And I have thoroughly

studied the game and I feel as if I have represented it in an

evolutionary way that will never be duplicated. I dug deep

down into the history and the mystery of the infamous pimp

game. Every man at some point wanted to be a pimp and a

player on some level and I have been fortunate to bring the

game to you. It has been an adventure and a life changing

experience and I'm going to leave you with a few brief words.

Live it. Breathe it. And achieve it. Because the world is yours!

And ready for the taking. Pimp long. And Pimp hard on every

corner, street, and boulevard. The world is yours for the taking!

This book is dedicated to a dear friend and brother who recently

passed away. You will forever be loved, missed, and cherished.

Thanks for all the loving memories, Mr. Devon Clemmons!

You have touched the lives of many people including your loving

children Blessing, Esssence, Gearralynn, Tyraile, and Tywaine.

And your first grandchild Jer'Robbie.

In loving memory of Mr. Devon Clemmons who graced us with

your presence from August 17, 1974 until June 19, 2021

Rest In Paradise My Brother!

ize.
NAC